The Great Depression

Researching American History

edited by
JoAnne Weisman Deitch

with an introduction by Kenneth M. Deitch
and essays by David C. King

Unemployed, destitute man, leaning against a vacant store.
(Photo by Dorothea Lange, courtesy of the FDR Library
Digital Archives)

Discovery Enterprises, Ltd.
Carlisle, Massachusetts

First Edition © Discovery Enterprises, Ltd., Carlisle, MA 2000

ISBN 1-57960-067-0

Library of Congress Catalog Card Number 00-191692

10 9 8 7 6 5 4 3 2 1

Printed in the United States of America

Subject Reference Guide:

Title: *The Great Depression*
Series*: Researching American History*
edited by JoAnne Weisman Deitch
with an introduction by Kenneth M. Deitch
and essays by David C. King

Nonfiction
Analyzing documents re: The Great Depression

Credits:

Cover photo: Oklahoma migrants, 1936, by Arthur Rothstein.

Other graphics are credited where they appear in the book.

Acknowledgments:

Special thanks to Kenneth M. Deitch and David C. King
for their informative introductory essays, and to
Janet Beyer, for her research and comments introducing
several excerpted documents.

More of these authors' work on The Great Depression can be
found in the following titles from the *Perspectives on History Series*
published by Discovery Enterprises, Ltd.:
The Great Depression: A Nation in Distress and *The Dust Bowl.*

Contents

About the Series

Researching American History is a series of books which introduces various topics and periods in our nation's history through the study of primary source documents.

Reading the Historical Documents

On the following pages you'll find words written by people during or soon after the time of the events. This is firsthand information about what life was like back then. Illustrations are also created to record history. These historical documents are called **primary source materials**.

At first, some things written in earlier times may seem difficult to understand. Language changes over the years, and the objects and activities described might be unfamiliar. Also, spellings were sometimes different. Below is a model which describes how we help with these challenges.

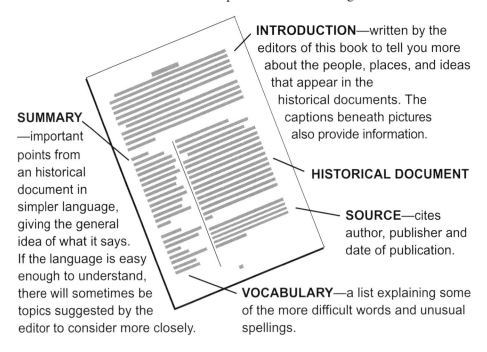

INTRODUCTION—written by the editors of this book to tell you more about the people, places, and ideas that appear in the historical documents. The captions beneath pictures also provide information.

SUMMARY —important points from an historical document in simpler language, giving the general idea of what it says. If the language is easy enough to understand, there will sometimes be topics suggested by the editor to consider more closely.

HISTORICAL DOCUMENT

SOURCE—cites author, publisher and date of publication.

VOCABULARY—a list explaining some of the more difficult words and unusual spellings.

In these historical documents, you may see three periods (…) called an ellipsis. It means that the editor has left out some words or sentences. You may see some words in brackets, such as [and]. These are words the editor has added to make the meaning clearer. When you use a document in a paper you're writing, you should include any ellipses and brackets it contains, just as you see them here. Be sure to give complete information about the author, title, and publisher of anything that was written by someone other than you.

INTRODUCTION
by
Kenneth M. Deitch

In the 1930s, America was truly a nation in distress. The previous decade—often called the Roaring Twenties—had been a generally prosperous and optimistic time, but in its closing months the economy began to falter. Not for over a decade would it genuinely recover. In its entirety, the economic catastrophe of the 1930s is known as the Great Depression. Its central feature was unusually large and long-lasting unemployment. Those in authority had no clear idea how to cure it.

The economy actually began its descent during the summer of 1929, but it is the crash of stock prices late in October that has come to symbolize the beginning of hard times. Throughout much of the 1920s, prices of stock traded on the New York Stock Exchange had risen at a pace that was reasonable, not excessive, given the strong economy. But during 1928, a high air of excitement took hold, and stock prices began racing upward. The enthusiasm—often called speculative fever—was fed by buying "on margin," that is, to a considerable extent with borrowed money. The momentum was destined not to last.

The downturn of stock prices began early in September of 1929, right after Labor Day. It was moderate at first, but starting late in October those who owned stock experienced a series of awful days, especially between the market's opening on "Black Thursday," October 24, and its close on "Black Tuesday," October 29. By mid-November, the Standard Statistics Index of stock prices had declined 39 percent from its highest value in September. As severe as losses had already been, more were coming as the depression worsened. When the index finally reached its low point in the summer of 1932, it had fallen 83 percent from September 1929's high point.

The suffering Americans experienced during the Great Depression extended far beyond the pain associated with the sharp decline in stock prices. Millions of ordinary people became unable to make a living. Unemployment in 1929 amounted to only 3.2 percent of the labor force, and then it began to grow. The two worst years were 1932, when the rate was 23.6 percent, and 1933, when it was 24.9 percent; in both years over 12 million people were unemployed. In the following years the situation was better, but throughout the remainder of the decade, it never became good. In 1939, the unemployment rate was still 17.2 percent.

Presenting the Great Depression through numbers is one way to tell about it, but mainly the story is one of human suffering. In *The Hungry Years: A*

Narrative History of the Great Depression in America, T. H. Watkins writes of a sense of despair "whose weight could bring the strongest man down in tears," and he passes on the sad story of a boy who later recalled that "to me the low point of the depression will always be the sight of my father...crying in the coal bin." The coal bin was empty.

People were deeply discouraged. Their mood is well expressed in the title of a song: "Brother, Can You Spare a Dime?" It also comes across in the words of A. N. Young, president of the Farmers' Union of Wisconsin, who told a Senate committee, "I am as conservative as any man could be, but any economic system that has in its power to set me and my wife in the streets, at my age—what can I see but red?"

Over a vast portion of America's Great Plains, farmers and their families became victims of another force above and beyond the crumbling economy: the weather. The years of depression were also years of drought, and by 1934 much of the land from the Dakotas to Texas and between the Mississippi River and the Rocky Mountains had turned from farmable soil to dust. The phrase "Dust Bowl" describes both the central core of this larger area and the conditions that drove so many farm families off the land. Often they moved westward. In telling the story of one such family, John Steinbeck spoke for all of them in his greatly admired novel, *The Grapes of Wrath*.

Herbert Hoover was less than a year into his presidency when the depression began, and he had certainly not been expecting it. Several months before his election he had spoken of soon being "within sight of the day when poverty will be banished from the nation." Once the depression began, he and members of his Administration made efforts to reverse it, but those efforts were insufficient.

Hoover was doomed to be a one-term President, and on election day in 1932 the voters turned to Franklin D. Roosevelt. He knew how important it was to give people hope for better times right at the outset. During the campaign, he had spoken of "a new deal for the American people." In his inaugural address on March 4, 1933, he began by focusing on people's spirits as he told the nation of "my firm belief that the only thing we have to fear is fear itself."

It would be many years before the Great Depression was over. It was President Roosevelt who led the nation out of it. While doing so, he and his Administration, working closely with Congress, created the New Deal, a collection of programs—Social Security is the most basic—that launched the modern era in the federal government's approach to economic policy. The era's central theme is the federal government's expanded role—expanded over what it was before the Great Depression—both in keeping the nation's economy on a stable path and in promoting the economic welfare of its citizens.

How it all began

The United States had too many banks, and too many of them played the stock market with depositors' funds, or speculated in their own stocks. Only a third or so belonged to the Federal Reserve System on which Hoover placed such reliance. In addition, government had yet to devise insurance for the jobless or income maintenance for the destitute. When unemployment resulted, buying power vanished overnight. Since most people were carrying a heavy debt load even before the crash, the onset of recession in the spring of 1930 meant that they simply stopped spending.

Together government and business actually spent more in the first half of 1930 than the previous year. Yet frightened consumers cut back their expenditures by ten percent. A severe drought ravaged the agricultural heartland beginning in the summer of 1930. Foreign banks went under, draining U.S. wealth and destroying world trade. The combination of these factors caused a downward spiral, as earning fell, domestic banks collapsed, and mortgages were called in. Hoover's hold the line policy in wages lasted little more than a year. Unemployment soared from five million in 1930 to over eleven million in 1931. A sharp recession had become the Great Depression.

Source: Hoover Presidential Library website: http://hoover. nara.gov/research

Summary:

The U.S. had too many banks, and they invested their depositors' money in the stock market. Most were not insured, and the government had no provision for helping unemployed people. So, when the crash came, people had to simply stop spending.

Drought hurt the farmlands; foreign banks failed; and, as earnings fell, the nation's banks collapsed. Unemployment grew to over 11 million.

Vocabulary:

called in = payment was
    demanded
debt = something owed
destitute = very poor
devise = create a plan for
drought = dry weather
expenditures = spending
hold the line policy = no
    changes in salaries
maintenance = keeping up
onset = the start
ravaged = destroyed
recession = falling off of
    business
reliance = trust
severe = harsh or serious
speculated = engaged in a
    risky financial venture

Police stand guard outside the entrance to New York's closed World Exchange Bank, March 20, 1931. (Courtesy of the Herbert Hoover Presidential Library and Museum)

People milling about, outside of bank, 1933. (Courtesy of the FDR Library Digital Archives, photo # 27-0642a.gif)

Hoover's Early Warning

In this statement covering both foreign and domestic economics, then-Secretary of Commerce Herbert Hoover voiced concerns regarding the inherent dangers of stock and real estate speculation.

"temper our optimism with...caution"

...Any business forecast must be simply an appraisal of the forces in motion at home and abroad, for and against progress. All signs indicate that if we will temper our optimism with a sprinkling of caution we shall continue our high level of prosperity over 1926.

The United States has produced and consumed more goods in 1925 in proportion to population than ever before in its history. Our standard of living has therefore been the highest in our history and is of course the highest in the world. This improvement, however, has been greater in the urban centres than in agricultural communities.

The dominant favorable factor in our outlook is our increased productivity, due to fundamental and continuing forces—such as the cumulation of education, the advancement of science, skill and elimination of waste.

Other favorable indications on the immediate horizon are that the stocks of commodities are moderate; there is employment for practically everyone; real wages are at a high level; savings are the largest in history and capital is therefore abundant; and the whole machinery of production and distribution is operating at a higher degree of efficiency than ever before. While wholesale prices for the year as a whole have averaged about 6% higher than for the previous year it is largely due to needed advance in prices of agricultural products.

continued on next page

Summary:

To make a business forecast, many things have to be considered. It appears that if we act cautiously, everything will continue to be good.

America's cities have been more prosperous than the farms.

We should increase productivity, improve education and science, and end waste.

Things are going well in employment, wages, savings, production, and distribution.

Vocabulary:

abundant = plentiful
appraisal = a set value
capital = wealth
consumed = used up
cumulation = addition
domestic = at home
dominant = ruling; main
elimination = removal
forecast = predict
inherent = built-in; part of
moderate = in reasonable limits
optimism = a hopeful outlook
previous = past

Summary:

We must be careful in several areas: real estate, stocks, installment buying, imports, farming, coal, and labor.

The farmers still have debt.

Construction has been doing well for three years. If we continue to be careful financially, things should improve even more in 1926.

Vocabulary:

accumulated debt = money owed

caution = being careful

commodities = farm and mining products

consequent = resulting

even keel = level position

extension = expanding

extortion = getting money by force or pressure

inevitable = unavoidable

inflation = increase in credit, resulting in a fall in value

instability = lack of firmness

installment buying = paying a little at a time

monopolies = companies with exclusive control of services or products

phases = aspects

prosperous = wealthy

optimism = the belief that good will prevail

unprecedented = unheard of before

There are some phases of the situation which require caution. Continuation of real estate and stock speculation and its possible extension into commodities with inevitable inflation; the over-extension of installment buying; the extortion by foreign Government-fostered monopolies dominating our raw material imports; the continued economic instability of certain foreign countries; the lag in recovery of certain major agricultural products; the instability of the coal industry; the uncertainties of some important labor relationships—all these are matters of concern. But, as said above, with caution we should continue a prosperous year over 1926.

Agriculture, while it is better than it was two years ago, still leaves the farmers with much accumulated debt....

The construction industries have played a very large part in the high business activity of the past three years. The volume of construction has been unprecedented during the past year with consequent great activity in the construction-material industries....

. . . .

On the whole, both our own country and the rest of the world face a more favorable outlook at this turn of the year than for a long time past. We, ourselves, however, need to be on our guard against reckless optimism. What we need is an even keel in our financial controls, and our growing national efficiency will continue us in increasing prosperity.

Source: Herbert Hoover, *The Commercial and Financial Chronicle,* January 2, 1926.

Hoover Urges Banking Reform

In his memoirs, Hoover discussed weaknesses he had seen in the nation's banking system. For one thing, only one third of the banks belonged to the Federal Reserve System. In addition, many of the larger banks speculated in stocks, indirectly using—and losing—their depositors' money.

"The worst part of the tragedy…"

…[T]he American people had been living for some years under an illusion of the absolute security to be had from the Federal Reserve System. We were slow to realize the dangers in our banking system.…

…I feel that our own banking and financial system was the worst part of the dismal tragedy with which I had to deal.

…Time and again from my first message to Congress, I urged the Congress to reform the banking laws to make depositors safe.

The public had become callous to bank failures because we had had over 4,000 such failures in the eight good years before the depression. More than 10,000 deposit institutions were to disappear in the five years after 1929, despite governmental props under the banking system.…

Source: Herbert Hoover, *Memoirs; The Great Depression,* Volume III. New York: The MacMillan Company, 1952.

Summary:

Americans thought our banks were safe, and didn't recognize the possible dangers in our system.

Our banking system was the worst part of this whole tragedy.

I tried to get Congress to reform our banking laws to protect deposits.

The public was used to failing banks because 4000 had failed before the depression even began. Ten thousand more disappeared after 1929, even though the government tried to help.

Vocabulary:

callous = unfeeling
dismal = miserable, gloomy
illusion = a false idea or image
institutions = long established organizations
memoirs = autobiography or recording of events
props = supports
security = safety

Summary:

Everyone knew someone who was facing hardship, but people kept their problems to themselves.

Organizations and individuals helped to distribute food.

In New York there were 82 bread lines and many men sold apples on street corners.

Hoover boasted that no one had starved.

The people who received relief sometimes had their rights taken away: like voting or sending their children to public schools. Some were even sent away from churches.

The State governments couldn't help. In 1929 Governor Roosevelt of New York organized a Welfare Department.

Vocabulary:

agony = pain
appropriations = money, set aside to help
civil rights = guaranteed rights of citizens
delinquents = overdue in their payments
denied = not allowed
improvised = made up

The Faces of Poverty

by Caroline Bird

…Everyone knew of someone engaged in a desperate struggle, although most of the agony went on behind closed doors. The stories were whispered.

. . . .

A Brooklyn convent put sandwiches outside its door where the needy could get them without knocking. St. Louis society women distributed unsold food from restaurants. Someone put baskets in New York City railroad stations so that commuters could donate vegetables from their gardens…. In San Francisco, the hotel and restaurant workers' union arranged for unemployed chefs and waiters to service elegant if simple meals to the unemployed….

…In New York City…there were enough hungry men without money to keep 82 badly managed breadlines going, and men were selling apples on every street corner….

"No one has starved," Hoover boasted.

…People who were on public relief were denied civil rights. Some state constitutions disqualified relief clients from voting…. In some places, village taxpayers' organizations tried to keep the children of tax delinquents out of the local schools. People suspected of taking public relief were even turned away from churches.

During the first and worst years of the Depression, the only public relief was improvised by cities. Appropriations were deliberately low. If funds ran out, so much the better. The poor would have to make another effort to find work….

State governments were not prepared to help. No state even had a Department of Welfare until Governor Franklin D. Roosevelt organized one for New York State in 1929. Cities begged for

12

temporary loans, banks were generally reluctant because cities did not have tax resources from which to pay back the money.... In January 1932, the New York City Department of Welfare did not have postage stamps on hand to distribute a million dollars raised and lent to the city by a committee of bankers.

Hoover kept insisting, no one starved....

Source: Caroline Bird, *The Invisible Scar.* New York: Longman, Inc., 1966.

Summary:

Cities begged for loans but the banks didn't have the money from taxes to give loans. In New York, the Welfare Department didn't have the money for stamps to mail out the million dollars it had raised to help people.

Vocabulary:

reluctant = unwilling
resources = wealth

New York food line (Courtesy of FDR Library, photo # 27-0639a)

"Hoovervilles"

As more and more people lost the ability to pay rents and mortgages, they were forced to leave their homes and improvise other shelter. Across the country shanty-towns, referred to as "Hoovervilles," sprung up.

Hundreds of quickly thrown-together shacks make up this Seattle Hooverville. (Special Collections, University of Washington Library)

Summary:

A few weeks ago, I visited a dump, in the middle of the steel mill district, which had three acres of waste land. It had all kinds of garbage, ash heaps, and junk. People live there in a shanty-town.

Vocabulary:

embankment = a supporting wall of earth

excrescences = human waste

flanking = on the side of

hamlets = little villages

incinerator = where garbage is burned

"God Bless Our Home"

A few weeks ago I visited the incinerator and public dump at Youngstown, Ohio. Back of the garbage house there are at least three acres of waste land, humpy with ash heaps and junk. The area is not on the outskirts but in the middle of the steel mill district with furnaces near-by, and the tube mills and factory stacks of Youngstown. The dump is a kind of valley with a railroad embankment flanking it. As you approach from the garbage house, certain excrescences compete in vision with the ash humps and junk. They appear more organized than the rest of the place, but one is not sure. When, however, you come close, there is no doubt but the dump is inhabited.

The place is indeed a shanty town, or rather a collection of shanty hamlets, for the separate blotches are not all in one place but break out

14

at intervals from the dump. Some of them are caves with tin roofs, but all of them blend with the place, for they are constructed out of it. From 150 to 200 men live in shanties. The place is called by its inhabitants—Hooverville.

I went forward and talked to the men; they showed me their houses. These vary greatly from mere caves covered with a piece of tin, to weather-proof shanties built of packing boxes and equipped with a stolen window-frame or an improved door. Some have beds and one or two a kitchen stove rescued from the junk heap, though most of the men cook in communal fashion over a fire shielded by bricks in the open.

· ·

This pitiable village would be of little significance if it existed only in Youngstown, but nearly every town in the United States has its shanty town for the unemployed, and the same instinct has named them all "Hooverville." The Pittsburgh unit has been taken under the wing of Father Cox—of Hunger March fame—who feeds the inhabitants at a soup kitchen in the cellar of his church, and who has supplied each shanty with a printed postcard: "God Bless Our Home." The largest Hooverville in the United States is in St. Louis, with a hovel population of 1200. Chicago had a flourishing one, but it was felt to be an affront to municipal pride and was ordered burned. The inhabitants were summarily told to get out, and thirty minutes later the "homes" were in ashes.

Source: Charles R. Walker, "*Relief and Revolution.*" The Forum, LXXXVIII (1932), pp. 73-4.

Summary:

Some of the houses are caves with tin roofs. About 150 to 200 men live here. They call it Hooverville.

I talked to some of the men, who showed me their houses. Some are furnished.

This village wouldn't be that important if it were the only one, but there are shanty-towns like this, for the un-employed, all over the U. S. The largest Hooverville, in St. Louis, has 1200 people. Chicago had one, too, but the city was ashamed of it, so they told the residents to get out, and then they ordered it burned down.

Vocabulary:

intervals = space between the times things are done

shanties = shabby huts or shacks

mere = simple

communal = together with the others in the community

Soup Lines and Bread Lines

In March 1932, as the Great Depression continued, people were forced to beg for food. Some met in soup kitchens and bread lines (community centers set up to distribute soup to hungry people) and Hoovervilles. Songs and poems grew out of this despair. The author of the following song is not known.

Soup Song

I spent twenty years in the factory,
I did everything I was told
They said I was faithful and loyal,
Now even before I get old: *CHORUS*

I saved fifteen bucks with my banker
To buy me a car and a yacht,
I went down to draw out my fortune,
And this is the answer I got: *CHORUS*

Source: Milton Meltzer, *Brother, Can You Spare a Dime?* New York: Facts on File, 1991, pp. 57-8.

A New York soup line (Library of Congress)

Dorothy Day and the Bread Lines

Dorothy Day spent her life taking care of people in need. She chose to live in poverty in the Lower East Side of New York, which was the headquarters for a newspaper she published, *The Catholic Worker*. During the Depression she became even more active and ran Hospitality Houses for the homeless.

An interview by Studs Terkel

...We didn't intend to have a bread line or a soup line come to the door. During the Seamen's Strike of 1937, six of them showed up.... We took in about ten seamen. We rented a store-front, while the strike lasted for three months. We had big tubs of cottage cheese and peanut butter, and bread by the ton brought in. They could make sandwiches all day and there was coffee on the stove.

While we were doing that for the seamen, one of the fellows on the Bowery [a section of New York noted for having many poor and homeless people] said, "What...are you doing down there feeding the seamen? What about the people on the Bowery? Nobody's feeding them." ...That's how the first bread line started.

Source: Studs Terkel, *Hard Times.* New York: Pantheon Books, 1970.

Summary:

We didn't plan to have a soup line or bread line. During the Seamen's Strike, people came to us for help. We rented a store and gave out food and coffee.

Then people asked us to help the hungry people in the Bowery, and that's how the first bread line started.

The People Speak Out

The Bonus Expeditionary Force

In 1924, Congress agreed to pay World War I veterans a bonus of $1 a day for each day of service in the U.S.; $1.25 per day for each day of service overseas. The bonus was to be paid in 1945. During the Great Depression the demand grew for immediate payment of the bonus, and many veterans or members of their families wrote emotional letters to Hoover's President's Committee for Unemployment Relief, headed by Walter Gifford. One of those letters follows.

Summary:

You told us to spend, but what should we use for money. We've been out of work for two years. Working people built homes and then had them taken away. Stop lying to us. Bankers and business leaders are greedy and are taking all the profits for themselves. President Hoover has tricked the soldiers out of their bonuses. He's a rich man and some of the men don't have $12 to their names.

Vocabulary:

bonus = an extra gift, in this case, more money

Expeditionary = in a march for battle

forgo = do without

slump = decline

veterans = someone who served in the armed forces

"stop bluffing us…"

Detroit, Michigan
September 29, 1931

Mr. Walter Gifford,

You have told us to spend to end the slump, but you did not tell us what to use for money, after being out of work for two years you tell us this. Pres. Hoover on the one hand tells the working man to build homes, and in the face of the fact nearly every working man has had his home taken off him…. Mr. Gifford why not come clean, and stop bluffing us. Tell us the reason of the depression is greed of Bankers and Industrialists who are taking too great of amount of profits…. The other day our Pres. Hoover came to Detroit and kidded the soldier boys out of their bonus. Pres. Hoover a millionaire worth about 12,000,000 dollars drawing a salary of 75,000 dollars per year from the government asking some boys to forgo their bonus some of them have not 12 dollars of their own….

J.B.

Source: Robert McElvaine, *Down and Out in the Great Depression: Letters from the Forgotten Man.* Chapel Hill, North Carolina: University of North Carolina Press, 1983.

Letters from the Forgotten Man

During the early years of the Great Depression, President Hoover received thousands of letters from average citizens, telling him what the depression was doing to them in their daily lives. Many letters also came from wealthy supporters who believed that things wouldn't be so bad if only the working class would try harder to survive.

When Franklin Roosevelt became president, almost a half million letters from men, women, and children arrived in the first few weeks. Letters addressed to the new president and to his wife, Eleanor, averaged around 6000 per day, for many years. (The FDR Library in Hyde Park, N. Y. has fifteen million of the letters.) An anonymous letter from a Chicago boy follows.

"Please you do something"

February 1936

Dear Mr. President,

I am a boy of 12 years. I want to tell you about my family. My father hasn't worked for 5 months. He went plenty times to relief, he filed out application. They won't give us anything. I don't know why. Please you do something. We haven't paid 4 months rent, Everyday the landlord rings the bell, we don't open the door for him. We are afraid that will be put out, been put out before, and don't want to happen again. We haven't paid the gas bill, and the electric bill, haven't paid grocery bill for 3 months. My brother goes to Lane Tech. High School. he's eighteen years old, hasn't gone to school for 2 weeks because he got no carfare. I have a sister she's twenty years, she can't find work. My father he staying home. All the time he's crying because he can't find work. i told him why are you crying daddy, and daddy said why shouldn't I cry when there is nothing in the house. I feel sorry for him. That night I couldn't sleep. The next morning I wrote this letter to you. in my room. Were American citizens and were born in Chicago, Ill. and I don't know why they don't help us. Please answer right away because we need it. Will starve Thank you. God bless you.

Summary:

I'm 12-years-old and my family needs help. My father hasn't worked for five months. We don't have enough money to pay the rent, and I don't want us to be thrown out of our apartment. We can't afford to pay our bills, and my brother can't pay the carfare to get to school. My sister can't find a job, and my father cries all the time, because things are so bad. I'm writing to you for help. We're American citizens, and we need help right away or we'll starve.

Vocabulary:

anonymous = the name of the person who wrote it is not known

relief = an agency that can help those in need

survive = live

Summary:

This is the first time in my life that I am asking for a favor.

Do you have any friend who is throwing away a size 40 or 42 coat? I haven't had a new coat for six years and I noticed the other day, when I was going to church, that mine is worn out. I only wear plain clothes. Any money we have has to go to our farming.

I hope you'll answer favorably.

Vocabulary:

discarding = throwing away or rejecting

Consider this:

When the economy is weak, and people don't have the money for the things they need, do you think prices should be lowered, so that poor people can buy what they really need? Who would be in control of this? Do you think poor people should get special discounts? Why or why not? Make up a system that you think is fair.

"Hoping for a favorable reply…"

Goff Kansas
May 10, 1935

Mrs. Franklin D. Roosevelt:
My Dear Friend:

For the first time of my lifetime I am asking a favor and this one I am needing very badly and I am coming to you for help.

Among your friends do you know of one who is discarding a spring coat for a new one. If so could you beg the old one for me. I wear a size 40 to 42 I have not had a spring coat for six years and last Sunday when getting ready to go to church I see my winter coat had several very thin places in the back that is very noticeable My clothes are very plain so I could wear only something plain. we were hit very hard by the drought and every penny we can save goes for seed to put in crop.

Hoping for a favorable reply.

Your friend Mrs. J.T.

An ad for women's coats. Prices were low, because few people could afford to buy anything.

The Women Do Their Part

Unlike the thousands of men who lost their jobs due to the depression, American women were used to being at home. They worked hard to stretch an ever-shrinking food budget, and read "ladies magazines" for suggestions on how to cope. For relief from the stress at home, the motion picture industry provided light-hearted entertainment from such super stars as Shirley Temple, Claudette Colbert, and Katharine Hepburn. At home, radio programs brought a mix of upbeat music, comedy shows, and solemn economic news.

The editorial pages of magazines like *The Ladies Home Journal* challenged women to do their part.

Purchasing Power

…If you do not exercise [your] purchasing power—that is, if you do not buy in your usual and reasonable fashion—you are cheating yourself of bargains and also in the end—you will cheat yourself of your income.

For, if no one buys beyond the bare necessities, the volume of business will go still lower and your income, no matter how solidly it seems to be founded, will come down in the chaos brought about by destructive thrift.

Cast a balance sheet on your own finances and see if you are financially hard up or only mentally hard up.

Source: Samuel Crowther, *The Ladies Home Journal.* March 1932.

Summary:

You should make good use of your purchasing power, and take advantage of any bargains.

Look over the expenses and income to see if the problems are real, or if you're just worried about spending.

Vocabulary:

budget = a plan for a cost of living expenses
chaos = confusion
solemn = serious
thrift = economical, spending very carefully
balance sheet = a statement showing finances

Lady removes pie from the oven. (FDR Library)

Although women had less money to spend, prices had dropped significantly, helping them to compensate for the reduction in family income.

Summary:

If a woman planned well and shopped well, she could feed a family of six very inexpensively.

Vocabulary:

compensate = to make up for

Making ends meet

With some creative shopping and cooking, a woman could feed a family of six on $5 a week, with milk at 10 cents a quart, a loaf of bread 7 cents, butter 23 cents a pound, and two pounds of hamburger for 25 cents....

Women shared inexpensive recipes:

Green Tomato Mincemeat

1 pk green tomatoes	2 t cinnamon
1/2 pk apples	1/2 t cloves
1/2 cup butter	1 box raisins
5 c white sugar	1 c cider vinegar

Grind tomatoes and apples, mix other ingredients, and cook for 2 hours. Place in 9-inch pie shells and bake 375 degrees. Makes 6 or 7 pies.

Source: Susan Ware, *Holding Their Own: American Women in the Depression.* Boston, MA: Twayne Publishers, 1982.

Consider this:

Figure out how much it would have cost for a family of four to eat a hearty breakfast. You determine the menu for the parents and the children.

Look in the newspaper's grocery ads (or go to the supermarket) and write down the cost of these items today.

Shopping for Groceries in the 1930s

sirloin steak (per lb.)	$.29
bacon (per lb.)	.22
chicken (per lb.)	.22
pork chops (per lb.)	.20
canned salmon	.19
milk (quart)	.10
1 dozen eggs	.29
bread (20 oz. loaf)	.05
coffee (per lb.)	.26
rice (per lb.)	.06
potatoes (per lb.)	.02
tomatoes (1 lb. can)	.09
onions (per lb.)	.03
Cornflakes (8 oz. box)	.08

The Women's Emergency Brigade at Flint, Michigan

by Janet Beyer

The unemployment of the depression added to continuing unfair labor practices, despite legislation to end such practices, and brought to a head the unrest among workers that had been brewing for several decades. Union organizers were able to make considerable progress, perhaps because the workers had so little to lose. Many employers, seeing in the depression the opportunity for lower wages and longer hours, fought the unions. One reason the automobile industry was particularly hurt by the depression was because people did not have money to buy cars.

In January 1937, the workers at the General Motors' Chevrolet plant in Flint, Michigan sat down on the job and would not leave the plant. This was one of the first "sit-down strikes" in the country. A committee chaired by Senator Robert La Follette had found General Motors guilty of corporate espionage and union-busting activities, in violation of New Deal legislation. This strike was one of the most crucial of the decade, and ended in victory for the workers.

On January 11, in below zero-weather, the company turned off the heat in one building. Strike supporters were forbidden to deliver food to the men.

This photo shows broken windows at General Motors in Flint during the sit-down strike of 1936-37. (Courtesy of the Michigan Historical Museum)

A battle waged between police and workers for three hours, ending in victory for the United Auto Workers. The new governor, Frank Murphy, sent in the National Guard but, sympathetic to the workers, refused to have them break the strike.

Three days later, 23-year-old Genora Johnson organized the Women's Emergency Brigade. It was made up of women who were willing to stand between the strikers and any force that would try to break the strike.

The strike, which spread to other GM buildings, lasted about six weeks. During the month the women had to march from one building to another to protect strikers in other sections of the plant. Women gathered from other cities to fortify the march.

Mary Heaton Vorse wrote about the Flint strike. She was a journalist and labor activist.

Summary:

In the hall there were many women with the Emergency Brigade, wearing red caps, and other groups wearing green or blue caps. These groups are springing up in many industries.

The EB is making history. Five hundred women are parading in support of the pickets. The pickets surround the plant.

Consider this:

Union members today also strike against management. Do you agree with the practice? Explain your reasoning.

Vocabulary:

Auxiliary = helper

Brigade = an organized group which works as a unit

contingent = part of a group

sympathizers = those who share feelings

The Brigade is organized

…The hall downstairs was full of red-capped women with EB (Emergency Brigade) on their arms. There was a large contingent of women with green tams and green armbands. They were members of the Detroit Women's Auxiliary, before whom members of the Flint EB spoke in Detroit. Already a thriving brigade is being organized that will wear blue tams. Brigades are springing up wherever cars are being made.

"Before we are through, there will be Emergency Brigades in steel, in rubber—wherever there are women's auxiliaries," a woman said.…

The Emergency Brigade Pickets

…Five hundred women are making history, since there is the first EB parade that has ever been held. The march around the business district was only the beginning. Soon the women were in cars on their way to the picket line around Fisher One.

Here they take part in one of the most amazing demonstrations this country has ever seen. Veterans in the labor movement insisted they had never seen anything like it. Six deep the picket marched around and around the factory. The picket line enfolded the great plant. Thousands of people on the picket line. Thousands of strike sympathizers looking on.

Source: Dee Garrison, ed., *Rebel Pen, the Writings of Mary Heaton Vorse.* New York: Monthly Review Press, 1985.

Writers Told the People's Stories

Life on the Farm

In the Tennessee Valley, overproduction and poor farm management caused an erosion of soil. The soil washed into the Mississippi River and the Gulf of Mexico. Overproduction of cotton crops in the south caused the price of cotton to drop to a point where it was not worth selling.

Without money people were not buying.

Tenant farmers, sharecroppers, and migrant farmers were the most severely affected. There was nothing to farm and no money for wages. They were not able to pay their rent, produce crops, or find work.

Writer James Agee and photographer Walker Evans documented the daily lives of three sharecroppers' families in Alabama. Below are excerpts from Agee's essays about the Gudgers, the Woods, and the Rickets families.

Tenant farmers harvested cotton and corn

Gudger—a family of six—lives on ten dollars a month rations during four months of the year. He has lived on eight, and on six. Woods—a family of six—until this year was unable to get better than eight a month during the same period; this year he managed to get it up to ten. Rickets—a family of nine—lives on ten dollars a month during this spring and early summer period.

This debt is paid back in the fall at eight per cent interest. Eight per cent is charged also on the fertilizer and on all other debts which tenants incur in this vicinity.

Working on third and fourth, a tenant gets the money from two thirds of the cottonseed of each bale: nine dollars to the bale. Woods, with a mule, makes three bales, and gets twenty-seven dollars. Rickets, with two mules, makes and gets twice that, to live on during the late summer.…

It is not often, then, at the end of the season, that a tenant earns enough money to tide him through the winter, or even appreciable part of it.

Summary:

The three families live on very small wages. When loans are paid back, there is very high interest to pay. By the time the summer is over, there is little if any money left to get them through the winter.

Vocabulary:
appreciable = noticeable
erosion = washing away of soil
incur = bring upon oneself
rations = fixed portion or share; a set allowance
sharecroppers = farmers who work the land for a share of the crop
tenant farmers = farmers who pay rent to farm
vicinity = area

Sharecroppers, weighing cotton, Texas, 1936. (Photo by Arthur Rothstein)

Summary:

The children's beds are rusty, damp, worn-out, and buggy. They are homemade. The mattresses are lumpy and the springs sag.

Vocabulary:

morbid = gruesome

sheaths = coverings

ticking = strong striped cloth used for covering mattresses and pillows

The Beds

The children's bed in the rear room has a worn-out and rusted mesh spring; the springs of the two beds are wire net, likewise rusty and exhausted. Aside from this and from details formerly mentioned, the beds may be described as one. There are two mattresses on each, both very thin, padded, I would judge, one with raw cotton and one with cornshucks. They smell old, stale and moist and are morbid with bedbugs, with fleas, and, I believe, with lice. They are homemade. The sheaths are not ticking, but rather weak unbleached cotton. Though the padding is sewn through, to secure it, it has become uncomfortably lumpy in some places, nothing but cloth in others…. The mattresses and springs are loud, each in a different way, to any motion. The springs sag so deeply that two or more, sleeping here, fall together at the middle almost as in a hammock.

Clothing

Louise: The dress she wore most was sewn into one piece of two materials, an upper half of faded yellow-checked gingham, and a skirt made of a half-transparent flour sack, and beneath this, the bulk of a pinned, I presume flour sack clout; and a gingham bow at the small of the back, and trimming at the neck. She has two other dresses, which are worn to Cookstown or for Sundays, and are, I imagine, being saved for school. They too are made painstakingly to be pretty, and as much as possible like pattern and ready-made dresses. During the week she is always barefooted and wears a wide straw hat in the sun. Her mother dresses her carefully in the idiom of a little girl a year or two littler than she is. On sundays she wears slippers and socks, and a narrow blue ribbon in her hair, and a many times laundered white cloth hat.

Junior: Ready-made overalls, one pair old, one not far from new, the newer cuffs turned up; a straw hat; bare feet, which are one crust of dew-poised sores; a ready-made blue shirt; a home-made gray shirt; a small straw hat. On sunday, clean overalls, a white shirt, a dark frayed necktie, a small, frayed, clean gray cap.

Burt: Two changes of cloths. One is overalls and one of two shirts, the other is a suit. The overalls are homemade out of pale tan cotton. One of the shirts is pale blue, the other is white; they are made apparently of pillowslip cotton. The collars are flared open: "sport collars," and the sleeves end nearer the shoulder than the elbow. The suit, which is old and, though carefully kept, much faded, is either a ready-made extravaganza or a hard-worked imitation of one. It is sewn together, pants and an upper piece, the pants pale blue, the upper piece white, with

Summary:

Louise wears an outfit made, in part, of sack cloth from a sack of flour. She has two other dresses for school and church. Her mother dresses her like a younger child would be dressed. She is barefoot during the week and wears socks and slippers on Sunday.

Junior wears overalls, and is barefooted. His feet have sores all over them. On Sunday he wears clean clothes, a tie, and a clean cap.

Burt has two sets of clothes. His faded old suit was either store-bought, or a carefully made copy of a ready-made suit.

Vocabulary:
extravaganza = a
    spectacular production
frayed = ragged
in the idiom of = in the
    manner of speech or
    custom associated with
    a certain type of person
painstakingly = carefully
pillowslip = cover for a
    pillow

Summary:

Katy and Flora are the same size and share their clothes with each other. They don't have any "Sunday clothes," so they wear whatever is the cleanest.

Vocabulary:

non-functional = not serving any purpose, not working

a small rabbit-like collar. There are six large white non-functional buttons sewn against the blue at the waistline.

…Katy and Flora Merry Lee are of the same size and use each others clothes. They have between them perhaps three dresses made of the sheeting, with short sleeves and widened skirts, and shirts or blouses made of thin washed flour sacking, and each has a pair of sheeting over-alls.…They have no "sunday" clothes; Sunday they wear the least unclean of these dresses, and a few heap pins, necklaces and lockets. During the week as well as on Sunday they sometimes tie dirty blue ribbons into their hair, and sometimes shoestrings.

Source: James Agee and Walker Evans, *Let us Now Praise Famous Men*. New York: Ballantine Walden Books, 1966.

Wife and children of a sharecropper in Washington County, Arkansas. (FDR Library Digital Archives)

The Dust Bowl
by David C. King

The "Dust Bowl" was a term used to describe both a region and a moment of history in the mid-1930s. After years of drought, a large area of the Great Plains was devastated by dust storms. Millions of tons of powdery dust that had once been rich topsoil were lifted into dense, dark clouds the people called "black blizzards." From the Dakotas in the North to Texas in the South, from the Mississippi River Valley in the East to the Rocky Mountains in the West, an area of 150,000 square miles became a desolate ruin. The parched land, stripped of its topsoil, turned into a dreary desert, incapable of supporting the homesteading families who had settled the region.

When the first dust storms struck in November, 1933, the farm families and townspeople were already reeling from the effects of the worst economic depression in the nation's history. During hard times in the past, a family with a little land could at least raise enough food to see them through. But the dust storms destroyed that traditional bit of security and people found themselves with nothing. In the hardest hit areas, more than sixty percent of the people were forced off the land.

Thousands of displaced farm families became migrants. They made their way to the cities or to other agricultural regions, hoping to find some way to survive. The largest numbers went to California in the hope that there they might rebuild their American dream. The government launched a variety of programs to offer short-term relief and long-term solutions. Some of the programs helped. Some didn't. The most devastating effects of the Dust Bowl did not end until the Second World War, when the increased demand for agricultural products and the resurgence of industries created both work and hope.

The dust storms, when they came, struck suddenly, beginning late in 1933. The conditions that led to those storms, however, had developed over nearly a century. It was the activity of farmers and ranchers over several decades that provided the recipe for disaster. Instead of plowing to follow the contours of the land, they plowed in straight lines. Millions of tons of precious topsoil were washed away into lakes, rivers, and streams. By 1930, the State of Iowa alone reported a loss of "550,000 tons of good surface soil per square mile, or a total of 30 billion tons" for the state.

While America and the world did not enter the Great Depression until after the Stock Market crash in 1929, the depression began in the 1920s for the nation's farmers. A government report, written in 1937, described what happened after the prosperous war years.

Overcropping and Erosion

Summary:

Farmers have been trying to grow crops on poor soil and have ruined good land because they have not protected it against erosion. Some didn't care about the future, and others couldn't afford to protect the land. The National Resources Board reported on millions of acres already destroyed by over-cropping and the destruction of topsoil, with many more acres that will continue to be destroyed.

The dry land of the Great Plains were over-planted and ruined. During World War I, the farmers had been encouraged to plow more and more land for planting—to help fill the need for wheat, but they didn't consider the consequences it would have.

Vocabulary:

allotted = a share given
conducive to = leading to
homesteading = farming
   public land given by the
   government
inevitable = unavoidable
outlay = money spent
precautions = care
provision = preparation
ravages = ruin caused by

"No provision was made…"

Not only have some farmers been trying to grow crops on hopelessly poor soil, but others have been ruining good land by practices conducive to soil erosion or have failed to take necessary precautions to protect land subject to erosion. Warnings of soil erosion have been heard in many areas for years, but these have been ignored by farmers who were too eager for immediate results to care about the future. Other farmers could not afford the outlay necessary to prevent erosion or had such limited acreages that they had no choice but to use their land to the full, regardless of the danger of over cropping. In 1934, the National Resources Board reported that the usefulness for farming of 35 million acres had been completely destroyed, that the top soil was nearly or entirely removed from another 125 million acres, and that destruction had begun on another 100 million acres.

Excessive cropping has been especially destructive on the dry land of the Western Great Plains, where quarter sections allotted to the settlers under the homesteading laws were too small for economic use of the land. The farmers were further led astray during the World War, when they were encouraged to break more and more sod in order to meet the world demand for wheat. No provision was made against the effects of the inevitable dry years, & vast acreages of dry soil were left unprotected by grass or trees against the ravages of wind & sun.

Source: Berta Asch & A.R. Magnus, "Farmers on Relief & Rehabilitation," *WPA Research Monogragh VIII.* Washington, D.C.: U.S. Government Printing Office, 1937, p. 12.

Soil erosion, Alabama, 1937. (Photo by Arthur Rothstein)

In the early 1930s, as the nation plummeted into the depths of the Great Depression, the plight of farm families steadily worsened. They were farming dangerously-eroded soil to raise crops that were constantly declining in price. One result was that more and more farmers were forced to become tenants, paying the landowner a percentage of their crop.

The prices farmers received for their products was so low that it often didn't pay to market them. As early as 1932, thousands of farm families had lost everything and took to the road. Some wandered aimlessly, hitchhiking from town to town in search of work. An Oklahoma resident described the situation to a Congressional hearing in 1932.

The plight of the farmers

...I talked to one man [who]...told me of his experience in raising sheep. He said that he had killed 3,000 sheep this fall and thrown them down the canyon, because it cost $1.10 to ship a sheep, and then he would get less than a dollar for it. He said he could not afford to feed the sheep, and he would not let them starve, so he just cut their throats and threw them down the canyon.

continued on next page

Summary:
One man killed 3,000 of his sheep because it cost him more to care for them and ship them than he would get for selling them.

Vocabulary:
aimlessly = without purpose
plight = distressing situation

Summary:

The roads in the West and South have many hungry hitchhikers. Campfires of the homeless are seen along the railroad tracks. Most were farmers who lost everything.

In some states, I saw cotton rotting in the fields because workers couldn't afford to pick it—the pay was so bad.

Because too much has been produced, and too little is used, 70% of the farmers in Oklahoma cannot pay the interest on their mortgages.

Vocabulary:
appalling = shocking
staggering = reeling
staple = regularly used or
    produced
underconsumption = used
    less than usual
untold = too much to be
    counted

The roads of the West and Southwest teem with hungry hitchhikers. The camp fires of the homeless are seen along every railroad track. I saw men, women, and children walking over the hard roads. Most of them were tenant farmers who had lost their all in the late slump in wheat and cotton....

In Oklahoma, Texas, Arkansas, and Louisiana I saw untold bales of cotton rotting in the fields because the cotton pickers could not keep body and soul together on 35 cents paid for picking 100 pounds. The farmers cooperatives who loaned the money to the planters to make the crops allowed the planters $5 a bale. That means 1,500 pounds of seed cotton for the picking of it, which was in the neighborhood of 35 cents a pound. A good picker can pick about 200 pounds of cotton a day, so that the 70 cents would not provide enough pork and beans to keep the picker in the field, so that there is fine staple cotton rotting down there by the hundreds and thousands of tons.

As a result of this appalling overproduction on the one side and the staggering underconsumption on the other side, 70 per cent of the farmers of Oklahoma were unable to pay the interests on their mortgages....

Source: Hearing before a Subcommittee of the Committee on Labor, House of Representatives, 72nd Congress, 1 Session, H.R. 206, Washington, D.C.: U.S. Government Printing Office, 1932, pp. 97-8.

Farm Foreclosures

When a farm family fell too far behind on its mortgage, the bank foreclosed and held an auction to sell off the family's farm animals, machinery, and equipment. At some of the auctions, crowds of sympathetic neighbors used a quiet pressure to make sure that no one bid a realistic price for any item. Sometimes the neighbors bought the stock or equipment for a few dollars, then gave it back to the family. Other times, as in the following account by a journalist, they forced the auctioneer to sell the items back to the farmer for ridiculously low amounts.

What is offered?

A raw, chilly day. The yard of the farm, churned black in a previous thaw, is frozen now in ruts and nodes. Where the boots of the farmers press, a little slime of water exudes, black and shiny. Through a fence the weather-bleached stalks of corn, combed and broken by the husking, stand ghostly in the pale air.… There are no leaders, no haranguers, no organization. In fact, this is the first affair of the sort in the county.

There is a movement toward the barns. The auctioneer mounts a wagon. The first thing offered is a mare. It is rather strange that livestock is offered first; the usual order is machinery first. The defaulting farmer stands silent holding the mare; he is a man almost elderly, quiet staid-appearing; and he stands embarrassed, smoothing the mane of the mare. The auctioneer goes through his regular cry. The mare is sixteen years old, sound except for a wire cut and a blue eye. What is he offered, what is he offered, what is he offered, does he hear a bid? He tries to make it sound like an ordinary sale. But the crowd stands silent, grim. At last someone speaks out. Two dollars. Two dollars! Unheard of, unbelievable, why she's worth twenty times that!

continued on next page

Summary:
Summarize this in your own words.

Vocabulary:
churned = stirred
defaulting = failing to pay when required
exudes = radiates
grim = stern, harsh
haranguers = people speaking a long time in a blustering manner
nodes = swellings
rigamarole = nonsense, or a foolish procedure
staid = sober, serious

Summary:

Continue to summarize this in your own words.

Vocabulary:

cultivator = a machine that prepares the soil for planting

disc-harrow = a heavy frame with discs, used to break up and level plowed ground

pulverizer = a machine that grinds into powder

The silence of the farmers is like a thick wall. The rigamarole of the auctioneer beats against it, and falls back in his face.... The farmer holding the mare stands with his head hanging. At last, without raising his eyes, he says, "Fifteen dollars." This is a new and distressing business to him, and he is ashamed to make a bid of less than that.

"…do I hear a twenty, a twenty, a twenty? Why she's worth twice that much." The auctioneer is still going through the make-believe. He keeps it up for five more minutes. A pause, and a voice speaks out, "Sell her…" It is not loud, but there is insistence in it, like the slice of a plow, with the tractor-pull of the crowd reinforcing it. The auctioneer hesitates, gives in. The silent, waiting crowd is too much. "Sold." After that there is less make-believe. Three more horses are offered. They are knocked down to the farmer, with no other bids, for ten dollars, eight dollars, a dollar and a half. The farmer is learning. The machinery comes next. A hay rack, a wagon, two plows, a binder, rake, mower, disc-harrow, cultivator, pulverizer. A dollar, fifty cents, fifty cents, a quarter, a half a dollar. Sold to the farmer. His means of livelihood are saved to him.

Source: Ferner Nunh, the *Nation*, March, 1911. Reprinted in *Brother, Can You Spare a Dime?* Milton Meltzer, New York: Facts on File, 1991, pp. 88-91.

AUCTION SALE
THURSDAY, JULY 30

Sale commences at 1:00 p. m. sharp

I will sell by public auction at my farm, 10 miles west of Charlson, 31 miles north-east of Watford City, on SE quarter, Sec.9-153-96, the following personal property:

Nine Head Horses

5—Good broke work horses (2 mares, 3 geldings)
2—Saddle horses—mares
2—Mare colts, 2 years old

Five tons hay.   Four sets harness.
17 horse collars.   One saddle.

FARM MACHINERY

1—10-20 McCormick-Deering tractor
1—McCormick-Deering d.d. grain drill
—Disc harrow
1—McCormick-Deering 22-in. separator
1—Single row corn cultivator
1—Garden cultivator
5—Wagons, 2 hay racks, wagon boxes
1—Sulky plow
1—Bob sled

1—Tractor plow
1—McCormick-Deering 8-ft. binder
1—McCormick-Deering mower, good as new.
1—John Deere hay rake, new
1—Boss harrow, 5 sections
3—Gang plows
1—Ford 1-ton truck
1—Harrow cart

Other articles and equipment too numerous to mention.

TERMS--CASH.   LUNCH AT NOON

No goods to be removed from premises till settled for.

GUY WILBER, OWNER

M. S. STENEHJEM, Auctioneer   First International Bank, Clerk.

Auction Poster from the Farm Security Adminstration. (Courtesy of the Library of Congress)

Black Blizzards and Flood Waters

The first dust storm struck the Great Plains on November 11, 1933. After three years of severe drought, the topsoil had become little more than a powdery dust. On that morning a fierce wind lifted what had once been farmland into swirling black clouds of dust. An estimated 300 million tons of soil were lifted into the air in the first of the "black blizzards." By afternoon the sun was blotted out in Chicago and a fine dust settled over everything—an estimated four pounds for every man, woman, and child in the city. The black clouds moved on, turning day to dusk in Albany two days later, then Boston, before depositing the last of the prairie soil in the Atlantic Ocean. The black blizzards continued through 1934, 1935, and into 1936.

Dust Storms

Lorena Hickok, an outstanding journalist hired as a "confidential investigator" for Harry Hopkins, who headed Roosevelt's Federal Emergency Relief Administration, was in Huron, South Dakota when the first dust storm hit. She wrote about it in a letter to Eleanor Roosevelt.

Summary:

I thought I had already seen everything bad that could happen until I saw that dust storm.

The wind howled all night and in the morning, you couldn't see the sun. Everything was in a brown fog.

We drove, but we had to turn back because we couldn't see.

Vocabulary:

desolation = laid to waste
fierce = violent, intense
gale = a strong wind
rapidly = quickly

"...you couldn't see the sun..."

I thought I'd already seen about everything in the way of desolation, discomfort, and misery that could exist, right here in South Dakota. Well, it seems that I hadn't. Today's little treat was a dust storm. And I mean a dust storm!

It started to blow last night. All night the wind howled and screamed and sobbed around the windows.

When I got up, at 7:30 this morning, the sky seemed to be clear, but you couldn't see the sun! There was a queer brown haze—only right above was the sky clear. And the wind was blowing a gale. It kept on blowing, harder and harder. And the haze kept mounting in the sky. By the time we had finished breakfast and were ready to start out, about 9, the sun was only a lighter spot in the dust that filled the sky like a brown fog.

We drove only a few miles and had to turn back. It got worse and worse—rapidly. You

Farmer and his sons walking through a dust storm in Cimarron County, Oklahoma, April, 1936. (Photo by Arthur Rothstein)

couldn't see a foot ahead of the car by the time we got back, and we had a time getting back! It was like driving through a fog, only worse, for there was that damnable wind. It seemed as though the car would be blown right off the road any minute. When we stopped, we had to put on the emergency brake. The wind, behind us, actually moved the car. It was a truly terrifying experience. It was as though we had left the earth. We were being whirled off into space in a vast, impenetrable cloud of brown dust.

They had the street lights on when we finally groped our way back into town. They stayed on the rest of the day. By noon the sun wasn't even a light spot in the sky any more. You couldn't see it at all. It was so dark, and the dust was so thick that you couldn't see across the street. I was lying on the bed reading the paper and glanced up—the window looked black, just as it does at night. I was terrified, for a moment. It seemed like the end of the world.

It didn't stop blowing until sundown, and now the dust has begun to settle. If you look straight up, you can see some stars!...

Source: Lorena Hickok, letter from Huron, SD, Nov. 11 & 12, 1933, in *One Third of a Nation*, pp. 91-2.

Summary:

It was like driving through fog, but the terrible wind made it worse. It blew the car so hard, we had to use the emergency brake. We felt like we were being blown into space in a cloud of dust.

We got back to town and we couldn't see anything. It seemed like the end of the world.

By sundown, the dust started to settle down and if you looked straight up, you could see some stars.

Vocabulary:

impenetrable = something you can't get through or penetrate

groped = felt blindly

Six months later, on May 11, 1934, a second black blizzard struck. Many said that this one was even more devastating than the first. Reporter Katherine Glover described the day in her book, *America Begins Again,* (p. 36).

Summary:

The second black blizzard hit the plains, causing devastating conditions.

Vocabulary:

debris = rubbish; dirt
momentous = important
moment

Consider this:

Compare the two eyewitness descriptions above, with Steinbeck's description from his novel.

Six months later a second storm hit…

May 11, 1934, although it passed with little notice, was almost as momentous in American history as April 6, 1917, when the United States entered the [First] World War. On that date a great dust storm blew across the continent from the plains of the West. Gray clouds choked the air for several hundred miles, day turned into night, and street lights were lighted in many cities. Railroad schedules were interrupted; roads were blocked; homes could not shut out the shifting sand; the soiling debris piled in stores, ruining thousands of dollars' worth of merchandise. Following in the wake of the storm, "dust pneumonia" took its toll in life.

The Grapes of Wrath

John Steinbeck, a native of California, met and wrote about many of the people who had been forced from their farms due to the dust storms and the depression, and migrated to California in hopes of a better life. Following is a brief quote from his classic book, *The Grapes of Wrath*:

"The dawn came, but no day. In the gray sky a red sun appeared, a dim red circle that gave a little light, like dusk; and as that day advanced, the dusk slipped back toward darkness, and the wind cried and whimpered over the fallen corn.

"Men and women huddled in their houses, and they tied handkerchiefs over their noses when they went out, and wore goggles to protect their eyes.

"When the night came again it was black night, for the stars could not pierce the dust to get down, and the window lights could not even spread beyond their own yards. Now the dust was evenly mixed with air, an emulsion of dust and air. Houses were shut tight, and cloth wedged around doors and windows, but the dust came in so thinly that it could not be seen in the air, and it settled like pollen on the tables and chairs, on the dishes. The people brushed it from their shoulders. Little lines of dust lay at the door sills."

Source: John Steinbeck, *The Grapes of Wrath*. Copyright 1939, renewed in 1967 by John Steinbeck, New York: Viking Press, 1976.

An Ironic Twist - Floods Strike in the East

Mississippi River Flood, 1936. (Photo by Arthur Rothstein)

As devastating as the dust storms were to the Great Plains, so were the extensive floods, east of the Mississippi River. Just as the western farmers had over-farmed their land, so had the eastern farmers cleared too much land for planting. When torrential rains hit the area in 1936, there was nothing to hold back the water, causing one of the most destructive floods in U. S. history. And, while western farmers and ranchers prayed for rain, 900 people in Ohio died in floods, and more than one half-million were driven from their homes.

In 1936 the Merrimac, Connecticut, Hudson, Delaware, Susquehanna, Potomac, Allegheny, and Ohio [Rivers] all went wild. The Potomac was up twenty-six feet at Washington and long barriers of sandbags protected government buildings. Pittsburgh was under ten to twenty feet of water and was without lights, transport, or power. The lives of 70,000,000 people [were] paralyzed. The food supply was ruined, the steel industry at a standstill.

Source: Stuart Chase, quoted in Ralph K. Andrist, ed., *The American Heritage History of the 20's and 30's.* New York: American Heritage Publishing Co., 1970, p. 307.

Summary:

In 1936, many eastern rivers flooded. In Washington, D.C., sand-bags were all that saved government buildings from the flooding. Pittsburgh was without lights, transportation and electricity. Food was not delivered. Steel industry workers couldn't work.

Keeping a Sense of Humor

An estimated 2.5 million people were displaced in the Great Plains states in the mid-1930s, and many flood victims also left their homes for a " new life." Even as they packed up their few meager belongings for an uncertain future on the road, the farm families had not lost their sense of humor. One Kansas farmer, for example, joked about "settin' on my porch and watching the neighbors' farms blow by." Two other examples of Dust Bowl humor:

Consider this:

Can you recall a situation where things were difficult, or sad, and someone reacted to it with a humorous quip? Does humor help to "ease the pain?"

Say it with a smile...

I'll plow next week. I reckon the farm'll blow back from Okla[homa] by then.

———

Well, we haven't lost everything. The wind blew the whole damn ranch out of state, but we ain't lost everything—we still have the mortgage.

Source: James D. Horan, *The Desperate Years.* NY: Bonanza Books, 1962, p. 165.

This cartoon was printed in The New York Times *in 1934. Artist unknown.* (Conde Nast Publications, Inc.)

The Migration Begins

In the mid-1930s, with their farms destroyed and no where else to turn, families took to the road in hopes of finding new opportunities. They piled their most important belongings on the family car or truck, if one was available, and headed off for the promised land. Those without transportation dragged their things on carts, wheelbarrows, and small wagons. Others jumped on railroad cars and headed to unknown destinations.

Some headed to the big cities and large towns, where they had relatives to put them up. Those unwilling to abandon their homes moved to neighboring towns to try to find work locally, usually without success. But the greatest number by far headed west to Washington, Idaho and Oregon on US Route 30, and on Route 66 to New Mexico, Arizona, and California.

By the late '30s, an estimated 300,000 of these migrants arrived in California. And, no matter where they had come from they were called "Okies."

The Joad family

John Steinbeck described the life of the Joad family in *The Grapes of Wrath,* as they traveled from Oklahoma to California.

"The cars of the migrant people crawled out of the side roads onto the great cross-country highway, and they took the migrant way to the West. In the daylight they scuttled like bugs to the westward; and as the dark caught them, they clustered like bugs near to shelter and to water. And because they were lonely and perplexed, because they had all come from a place of sadness and worry and defeat, and because they were all going to a new mysterious place, they huddled together; they talked together, they shared their lives, their food, and the things they hoped for in the new country. Thus it might be that one family camped near a spring, and another camped for the spring and for the company, and a third because two families had pioneered the place and found it good. And when the sun went down, perhaps twenty families and twenty cars were there.

"In the evening a strange thing happened: the twenty families became one family, the children were the children of all. The loss of home became one loss, and the golden time in the West was one dream. And it might be that a sick child threw despair into the hearts of twenty families, of a hundred people; that a birth there in a tent kept a hundred quiet and awestruck through the night and filled a hundred people with the birth-joy in the morning. A family which the night before had been lost and fearful might search its goods to find a present for a new baby. In the evening, sitting about the fires, the twenty were one."

*Tenant farmer moving, Hamilton County, Tennessee, 1936. (*Photo by Arthur Rothstein)

Migrant to Oregon, from South Dakota, 1936. (Library of Congress)

Migrant Workers in the Promised Land
by David C. King

The Okies quickly found that they were not welcome in California. To the people of the state, these penniless newcomers looked—and were—dirty, their tattered clothes covered with the dust of travel and roadside camps. Their faces wore a haunted, hungry expression that frightened people. Los Angeles even tried to keep them out with "bum blockades" manned by armed deputies, until the courts told them it was illegal to turn back the newcomers.

While some Okies moved to the cities, most headed for the farm fields, where huge agricultural corporations grew cash crops that required seasonal pickers. Most migrant families lived in miserable conditions. They cooked over campfires, drew water from polluted irrigation ditches, and slept under any scraps of shelter they could construct. One government inspector told of finding forty-one people living in a two-room cabin.

Woody Guthrie said it all in his songs...

Woody Guthrie, who later became one of the nation's best-known composers of folk songs, captured the essence of the migrants' problems awaiting them in California. Following are the lyrics from one of his popular songs.

Lots of folks back east, they say,
    leavin' home every day,
Beatin' the hot old dusty way to the California line;
'Cross the desert sands they roll,
    gettin' out of that old Dust Bowl,
They think they're goin' to a sugar bowl,
but here is what they find:
Now the police at the port of entry say,
"You're number fourteen thousand for today."
Oh, if you ain't got the do-re-mi, folks,

If you ain't got the do-re-mi,
Why you better go back to beautiful Texas,
Oklahoma, Kansas, Georgia, Tennessee.
California is a garden of Eden,
A paradise to live in or see,
But believe it or not, you won't find it so hot,
If you ain't got the do-re-mi.

Summary:

Lots of people leave every day for California. They want to get away from the Dust Bowl, so they head for the "sugar bowl," a sweet place, California. But the police in California are trying to keep the migrants out, because so many arrive each day that they've set quotas (limits.)

So, if you don't have any money ("do-re-mi"), you better go back home. California is a real paradise, but not if you're broke.

A year in the life of a typical migrant

Consider this:

This worker went from one job to another, wherever he could find work. Which job paid the best? Which sounds like the most difficult?

Vocabulary:

victrolas = phonographs

July-October 1932. Picked figs at Fresno, Calif., and vicinity. Wages, 10 cents a box, average 50-pound box. Picked about 15 boxes a day to earn $1.50; about $40 a month.

October-December 1932. Cut Malaga and muscat (table and wine) grapes near Fresno. Wages, 25 cents an hour. Average 6-hour day, earning $1.50; about $40 a month.

December 1932. Left for Imperial Valley, Calif.

February 1933. Picked peas, Imperial Valley. Wages, 1 cent a pound. Average 125 pounds a day. Earned $30 for season. Also worked as wagon-man in lettuce field on contract. Contract price, 5 cents a crate repack out of packing house; not field pack. This work paid 60 cents to $1 a day. On account of weather, was fortunate to break even at finish of season. Was paying 50 cents a day room and board.

March-April 1933. Left for Chicago. Stayed a couple of weeks. Returned to California two months later.

May 1933. Odd-jobs on lawns, radios, and victrolas at Fresno. Also worked as porter and handy man.

June 1933. Returned to picking figs near Fresno. Wages, 10 cents a box. Averaged $1.50 a day, and earned $50 in two months.

Source: John N. Webb, research report quoted in Milton Meltzer, *Brother, Can You Spare a Dime?* New York: Facts on File, 1991, pp. 97-8.

The Young Vagabonds

Many teenagers headed out on their own, without the companionship or support of their families. Some were escaping poverty, others were escaping the law. Reporter Maxine Davis described the situation in a magazine article.

...being told endlessly to "move on"

Two hundred thousand unwanted, homeless boys—with a scattering of girls, are wandering about the United States, meagerly fed, scantily clothed, being told endlessly to "move on."

No use to go home even if they could get there—for home offers even less in sustenance than the open road. No jobs to be had regularly. Few beds to sleep in, except the railroad tracks.

Here are Red and Mike and Tom. They met in the box car where we find them—traveling west on the Southern Pacific Railroad. After a desultory conversation they found they were all fugitives from the Detention House in New Orleans, which promptly made them pals. There are five others in the box car. The sun beats down and the alkaline dust gives them the appearance of cement workers. As the train is one of the very longest transcontinental freights there are,...about seventy-five such boys on board....

These...boys are typical of the many roaming with enforced aimlessness about the land. They are good boys. They would work if there were work to do. They don't drink. They don't steal. They are shy, suspicious and miserable. This army of boys follows a line of march chiefly from the Eastern States to the South and Southwest. They belong nowhere. Nobody wants them. Usually they are the children of families in which the wage earners are out of work and where there are younger brothers and sisters to be fed and housed....

Source: Maxine Davis, *Ladies Home Journal*, September 1932.

Summary:

Two hundred thousand boys and girls are wandering around the country, poorly fed and clothed. They are told to move on.

They can't go home because food and job opportunities are even worse at home.

Some boys on a train found out that they had all fled a juvenile detention facility in New Orleans, so they became pals. As they ride along in the boxcar, covered with dust, they give the appearance of cement workers.

They're "good" kids, who'd like to work if they could. Now, they don't belong anywhere, and no one wants them.

Vocabulary:

aimlessness = no purpose
desultory = disconnected
enforced = imposed
fugitives = those fleeing
    from justice; escapees
meagerly = inadequately
scantily = barely enough
sustenance = food or
    means of livelihood

Looking Ahead to Better Times

by JoAnne Weisman Deitch

The effects of the Great Depression were devastating to the people of the United States and to people around the world. Although President Hoover had tried to ease the economic problems by shoring up banks with loans from the government, his hope that the money would "trickle down" to businesses and therefore to their employees did not materialize. Hoover believed that Americans should maintain their self-reliance and not receive relief from the Federal government.

When the election of 1932 came around, millions of Americans were at the end of their rope. They looked at Franklin Delano Roosevelt as a long-awaited change…not only in attitude, but in the level of energy and spirit of rebirth he might bring to the nation. Roosevelt campaigned on one issue alone: "…aid must be extended by government…as a matter of social duty." He had already proven as governor of New York that relief programs could provide jobs for the unemployed. He was willing to push for similar programs on a national scale.

Roosevelt won the election easily, carrying forty-two of the forty-eight states. Addressing the Democratic convention in Chicago, he made a promise to restore America to its previous greatness. "I pledge you, I pledge myself, to a new deal for the American people."

Herbert Hoover and Franklin D. Roosevelt on inauguration day, March 4, 1933. (Used with permission. FDR Library and Museum photo #09-1752a.)

What Had Happened to the American Dream?

by David C. King

For the victims of the Dust Bowl—as for all those who suffered during the Great Depression—one of the overriding emotions was one of bewilderment. What had happened to the American dream, which had once seemed so attainable? How could there be so much hunger and misery in the land of plenty? What had become of the rewards for those who worked hard and lived decently? And how could people maintain a sense of community, or of neighbor helping neighbor, when it seemed that everyone was down and out?

President Franklin Roosevelt, and the men and women who formed his New Deal administration, were among the first to see that massive government action was needed. In simple terms, Roosevelt stated what amounted to a major shift in American thinking: "If private...endeavor fails to provide work for willing hands and relief for the unfortunate, those suffering through no fault of their own have a right to call upon the government for aid." The New Deal was an effort to respond to that call.

The Government's Search for Solutions

When Roosevelt took the oath of office as president in March, 1933, he did not have a specific set of plans for addressing the massive, complex problems of the Great Depression. He promised a "New Deal for all Americans," but he was not sure what that would consist of. Harry L. Hopkins, one of FDR's closest advisors, may have summed up the New Deal philosophy best when he said, "I am for experimenting, trying out schemes which are supported by reasonable people and see if they work. If they do not work, the world will not come to an end."

And experiment they did, launching a dizzying array of programs with two goals in mind: first, to relieve as much human suffering as possible, as rapidly as possible; second, to try to correct some of the underlying conditions that had led to that suffering.

The depression [had] brought America to a crossroads. A society based on a belief in "rugged individualism" had broken down. For the first time in our history, people came to the realization that only the national government had the resources to provide some relief.

Note: You will find a continuing discussion of the relief measures that were implemented during this period in American history in *The New Deal,* part of the *Researching American History Series,* edited by JoAnne Weisman Deitch, Carlisle, MA: Discovery Enterprises, Ltd., 2000.

Research Activities/Things to Do

- Compare and contrast the hardships felt by people who lived in the cities with people who lived on farms during the Great Depression.

- Visit your local bank and ask one of the customer service people to tell you about the safeguards for depositors. You may want to call first to make an appointment. Was the bank operating in the 1930s?

- Interview a grandparent, a nursing home resident, or a neighbor who lived through the Great Depression and ask them about it. Prepare your questions in advance.

- If you had been a member of one of the farm families hit by the dust storms during the '30s, do you think you would have wanted to stay on your farm or leave? Why or why not? What would you lose by leaving? What would you gain?

- Above is a photo of Buchanan's general store at Hovey, Indiana, open for business after the flood. Note furniture placed on roof to protect it from flood waters. Write a short story or journal entry about your experience in one of the 1936-7 floods. (Photo by Russell Lee, 1937 Feb.)

- The vagabond boys depicted in the article on page 45 were part of a new homeless class of people in the U. S. How does the portrayal of these boys compare to your concept of runaway teens today? Explain.

- Although women had received the right to vote in 1920, the Great Depression slowed their progress in the area of equal opportunity. Explain why.

- Being a conscientious and budget-minded housewife was the order of the day in the 1930s. Find examples of cost-saving practices that helped families get by during these tough economic times. You may want to go to the library to read some old magazine articles, or interview women who lived during the Depression.

- Why was it even more difficult for women and Blacks to find work during the Depression that it was for white men?

- Migrant farmers were forced to live in makeshift housing, with little income for food and clothing. In the cities, unemployed men who lost their housing had to move into shanty-towns on vacant land or at city dumps. Write an essay or short story about your family having to spend a year living like this. Try to get some good details from the primary sources that you read. It will also be helpful to study some of the many excellent photographs from this period.

- In the late 1920s, many people got very involved in stock and real estate speculation. Although they made a lot of money at first, when the stock market crashed in 1929, many lost almost everything they had. Today, many families in the U. S. invest in the stock market, too. Find out whether such investments are safer now (in terms of avoiding a possible crash), and why, or why not? If your school has an investment club, you might want to join it to learn more about the stock market. Or, if your parents invest, ask them about it.

- When the nation was in the depths of the Great Depression, people turned to the entertainment industry to give them some relief from their feelings of despair. Make a list of the most popular movies, movie stars, comic books, games, radio shows, etc., that helped to get people through the Depression. (The internet is a good source for your research, and also, many of the history books which are available.)

- Some people think that *The Wizard of Oz* is, on another level, about the Great Depression. What does the symbolism stand for? Explain things like the tornado, Toto, the yellow brick road, the witch, the wizard, and Oz.

Sample Cartoon

Mopey Dick and the Duke, by Denys Wortman

"Here, put this toothpick in your mouth, Mopey, and the other guys will think we had something to eat."

• Use the Cartoons Worksheet to analyze this cartoon.

Analyzing Cartoons Worksheet

Based on Worksheet from *Teaching with Documents,*
National Archives and Records Administration

1. **Describe the action taking place.**

2. **In your own words, explain the message.**

3. **List the key objects in the cartoon and describe what each symbolizes.**

    Object   *Symbolizes*

4. **How does the caption (if there is a caption) tie in with the picture?**

5. **If there are words in the illustration area of the cartoon, how do they enhance or relate to the caption?**

6. **What is the cartoonist's point of view?**

7. **Who do you think the intended audience is?**

8. **What is the significance of any dates or numbers that appear?**

9. **Are the people in the cartoon caricatures of famous people or just representative of average people or stereotypes of a group?**

Sample Songs

• Use the Songs/Poems Worksheet to analyze these songs.

Source: *Voices from the Dust Bowl: The Charles L. Todd and Robert Sonkin Migrant Worker Collection, 1940-1941.* Found at website: http://memory.loc.gov/cgi-bin/query/r?ammem/todd:@field

Some More Greenback Dollar
Indio Newspaper, 1940

I don't want your little rag houses
I don't want your navy beans
All I want is a greenback dollar
For to buy some gasoline.
The scenery here is gettin' rusty
I'll go further up the line
Where the fields are green and purty
It will satisfy my mind
We don't want to be a burden
On the people of this land
We just want to earn our money
And you people know we can.
So goodbye my friends and neighbors
We are on the tramp
Many thanks to all officials
Of this migratory camp.

Why We Come To Californy
Flora Robertson Shafter, 1940

Here comes the dust-storm
Watch the sky turn blue.
You better git out quick
Or it will smother you.
Here comes the grasshopper,
He comes a-jumpin' high.
He jumps away across the state
An' never bats an eye.
Here comes the river
it sure knows its stuff.
It takes our home and cattle,
An' leaves us feelin' tough.
Californy, Californy,
Here I come too.
With a coffee pot and skillet,
I'm a-comin' to you!

Analyzing Songs/Poems Worksheet

1. **Type of song document:**
   ❏ Sheet music   ❏ Recording   ❏ Printed Lyrics only
   ❏ Other_____

2. **Time period from which the song or poem comes:**

3. **Date(s) on Song:**
   ❏ No Date   ❏ Copyright

4. **Composer:**   **Lyricist:**   **Poet:**

5. **For what audience was the piece written?**

6. **Key Information** (In your opinion, what is the message of the song/poem?)

7. **Do you think the song/poem was spontaneously written?**

8. **Choose a quote from the piece that helped you to know why it was written:**

9. **Write down two clues which you got from the words that tell you something about life in the U. S. at the time it was written:**

10. **What is the mood of the music or poetry?**

11. **Do you think the song/poem was used for propaganda? If so, describe the propaganda:**

12. **Does the wording have any "secret message" or symbolic meaning?**

Sample Chart

Source: Cabell Phillips, *From the Crash to the Blitz: 1929-1939,* New York Times Company, New York: 1969, p. 414.

	1935*	%	1960**	%
Average annual income	$1,348	—	$5,368	—
Food and alcoholic beverages	472	35.4	1,406	26.0
Housing, heat, utilities, furnishings, etc.	456	33.3	1,584	29.5
Clothing	136	10.2	550	10.4
Automobile purchase and operation	73	5.5	696	13.0
Medical care	53	4.0	345	6.6
Recreation, reading, tobacco	72	5.4	—	—
Recreation, reading, education	—	—	326	6.0
Taxes	5	.4	666	12.0
Miscellaneous expenses	5	.4	118	2.2

* From "How American Buying Habits Change," U.S. Department of Labor, p. 44.
** From "Handbook of Labor Statistics, 1968," U.S. Department of Labor, p. 283.

- How much money would be left after a household made all of the purchases in 1935? and in 1960?

- Why might the descriptions of certain items have changed from 1935 to 1960? (See lines 7 and 8)

- Which category increased the most in the two time periods? Which decreased the most? (Use dollar amounts, and then look at the % figures.)

- Make your own column for 1999. First, estimate what you think the figures might be. Then, call, write or e-mail the Department of Labor for the actual figures. Were you close? What was "off" the most?

Analyzing Charts/Graphs Worksheet

1. **Identify the chart or graph:**

   a. Type:
   - ❏ Pictograph
   - ❏ Bar graph
   - ❏ Pie chart
   - ❏ Line graph
   - ❏ Diagram
   - ❏ Table
   - ❏ Time line
   - ❏ Schedule

   b. Title: Source:

   c. Purpose:

2. **What groups does the chart or graph represent?**

3. **What else is represented?**
   - ❏ Geographic information
   - ❏ Time period(s)
   - ❏ People
   - ❏ Other_____

4. **Summarize the data in a complete sentence:**

5. **Draw conclusions from the data:**

6. **Synthesize/Evaluate the data:**

   a. Develop a hypothesis about trends, patterns, or changes indicated by the data:

   b. Write a question about the chart/graph:

   c. What related historical information could add to your understanding of it?

   d. Make a prediction, based on your analysis of the data:

   e. Describe the event or issue that this chart/graph helps to explain:

7. **Make a different type of chart or graph based on data found.**

Suggested Further Reading

Companion Literature Compiled by Ellin Rossberg

The books listed below are suggested readings in American literature, which tie in with the *Researching American History Series*. The selections were made based on feedback from teachers and librarians currently using them in interdisciplinary classes for students in grades 5 to 12. Of course there are many other historical novels that would be appropriate to tie in with the titles in this series.

The Great Depression and The Dust Bowl

The Grapes of Wrath, John Steinbeck - M/HS

I Know Why the Caged Bird Sings, Maya Angelou - HS

Riding the Rails: Teenagers on the Move During the Great Depression, Errol Lincoln Uys - M/HS

Bud, Not Buddy, Christopher Paul Curtis - EL/M

Roll of Thunder, Hear My Cry, Mildred Taylor - M

Hard Times, Studs Terkel - HS

No Promises in the Wind, Irene Hunt/James Lincoln - M

Web Sites

National Archives site featuring Depression-era artwork, interviews, etc., at: http://www.nara.gov/exhall/newdeal/newdeal.html

The Franklin D. Roosevelt Library and Museum web site at: http://www.fdrlibrary.marist.edu/images/photodb/

Quotes and photos of Eleanor Roosevelt can be found at this site: http://newdeal.feri.org/eleanor

Hoover Presidential Library website: http://hoover.nara.gov/research

The Library of Congress' American Memory site: http://memory.loc.gov/

Another good site: http://www.spartacus.schoolnet.co.

For information on these and other titles from Discovery Enterprises, Ltd., call or write to: Discovery Enterprises, Ltd., 31 Laurelwood Drive, Carlisle, MA 01741 Phone: 978-287-5401 Fax: 978-287-5402